Friends Indeed:
Thoughts on Friendship

Edited by Alison Bing

BARNES
& NOBLE
BOOKS
NEW YORK

The quotes in this book have been drawn from many sources, and are assumed to be accurate as quoted in their previously published forms. Although every effort has been made to verify the quotes and sources, the publisher cannot guarantee their perfect accuracy.

2003 Barnes & Noble Books

ISBN 0-7607-4063-1

Printed and bound in the United States of America

M 9 8 7 6 5 4 3 2

GREETINGS, FINE FRIEND,

Here's a little friendly advice for you . . . no, not the kind snitches get in mob movies when they're already fitted for cement shoes. On the contrary—this is the wise counsel that may just save you from a fate worse than cement shoes, brought on by one of those trick questions friends inevitably ask.

You know the ones:

- You do remember it's my birthday today, right?
- Does it look like my hair is thinning?
- So what do you think about my new boy/girlfriend?
- Can you change my cat's litter while I'm away?

Fear not: This book gives you the power to disarm any such question with a brilliant insight on friendship from a great thinker. Your friend will be duly impressed, and with any luck you can evade the original question and still end up on the convivial side of the friend-or-foe equation. All may be fair in love and war, but friendship takes some diplomacy—so a few well-chosen words will always come in handy.

May friendly thoughts always be with you, even if you have to borrow one now and again.

—Alison Bing

A Friend's Role

Friendship is unnecessary, like philosophy, like art…. It has no survival value; rather is one of those things that give value to survival.

—C. S. LEWIS, *The Four Loves*

The bird a nest,
the spider a web,
man friendship.

—WILLIAM BLAKE, "Proverbs of Hell,"
The Marriage of Heaven and Hell

The only ship worth a damn is friendship.

—MONTGOMERY BURNS, *The Simpsons*

Friendship is the hardest thing in the world to explain. It's not something you learn in school. But if you haven't learned the meaning of friendship, you really haven't learned anything.

—attributed to MUHAMMAD ALI

I know there are people in this world who do not love their fellow man, and I hate people like that!

—TOM LEHRER, "Songs By,"

We regard our living together not as an unfortunate mishap warranting endless competition among us, but as a deliberate act of God to make us a community of brothers and sisters jointly involved in the quest for a composite answer to the varied problems of life.

—attributed to STEVEN BIKO

A friend may well be reckoned the masterpiece of Nature.

> —Ralph Waldo Emerson, *Essays: First Series*

I suppose there is one friend in the life of each of us who seems not a separate person, however dear and beloved, but an expansion, and interpretation, of one's self, the very meaning of one's soul.

> —Edith Wharton, *A Backward Glance*

Friendship is the only cement that will ever hold the world together.

> —Woodrow Wilson,
> in a 1919 speech for the League of Nations

We are here on earth to do good to others. What the others are here for, I don't know.

> —attributed to W. H. Auden

And all people live, not by reason of any care they have for themselves, but by the love for them that is in other people.

—attributed to LEO TOLSTOY

What is a friend? A single soul dwelling in two bodies.

—ARISTOTLE

She is a friend of my mind. She gather me, man. The pieces I am, she gather them and give them back to me in all the right order.

—TONI MORRISON, *Beloved*

Kismet

The meeting of two personalities is like the contact of two chemical substances; if there is any reaction, both are transformed.

—CARL JUNG, *Modern Man in Search of a Soul*

Take us for example... Why should we have met? How did it happen? It can only be that something in our particular inclinations made us come closer and closer across the distance that separated us, the way two rivers flow together.

—GUSTAV FLAUBERT, *Madame Bovary*

Adapt yourself to the things among which your lot has been cast and love sincerely the fellow creatures with whom destiny has ordained that you shall live.

—MARCUS AURELIUS, *The Meditations*

Two may talk together under the same roof for many years, yet never really meet; and two others at first speech are old friends.

—MARY CATHERWOOD,
"Marianson," *Mackinac and Lake Stories*

She felt the natural ties of affinity, rather than the conventional blind ties of the blood.

—NADINE GORDIMER, "La Vie Bohème," *Face to Face*

Each friend represents a world in us, a world possibly not born until they arrive, and it is only by this meeting that a new world is born.

—ANAÏS NIN, *The Diary of Anaïs Nin, Vol. 2*

Making Friends

My mother used to say that there are no strangers, only friends you haven't met yet. She's now in a maximum security twilight home in Australia.

—DAME EDNA EVERAGE, *Dame Edna Everage and the Rise of Western Civilization*

You can make more friends in two weeks by becoming interested in other people that you can in two years by trying to get other people interested in you.

—DALE CARNEGIE, *How To Win Friends and Influence People*

Friendship is always a sweet responsibility, never an opportunity.

—KAHIL GIBRAN, *Sand and Foam*

What is uttered from the heart alone
Will bend the hearts of others to your own.

—JOHANN WOLFGANG VON GOETHE, *Faust*

A timid young woman named Jane
Found parties a terrible strain;
With movements uncertain
She'd hide in a curtain
And make sounds like a rabbit in pain.

—EDWARD GOREY, *The Listing Attic*

There was a definite process by which one made people into friends, and it involved talking to them and listening to them for hours at a time.

—REBECCA WEST, *The Thinking Reed*

I enjoy talking to you. Your mind appeals to me. It resembles my own mind, except that you happen to be insane.

—GEORGE ORWELL, *1984*

I prefer to be true to myself, even at the hazard of incurring the ridicule of others, rather than to be false, and to incur my own abhorrence.

—FREDERICK DOUGLASS,
The Narrative of the Life of Frederick Douglass

Friendship with oneself is all-important, because without it one cannot be friends with anyone else in the world.

—ELEANOR ROOSEVELT

It is far more impressive when others discover your good qualities without your help.

—MISS MANNERS (A.K.A. JUDITH MARTIN),
as quoted in *Reader's Digest*

The only way to have a friend is to be one.

—Ralph Waldo Emerson, *Essays: First Series*

What a delight it is to make friends with someone
you have despised!

—Sidonie Gabrielle Colette,
Earthly Paradise: An Autobiography

If you judge people, you have no time to love them.

—attributed to Mother Teresa

Choose your friends carefully. Your enemies will
choose you.

—attributed to Yassir Arafat

Love is the only force capable of transforming an
enemy into a friend.

—Rev. Dr. Martin Luther King, Jr.,
Strength to Love

Bonding Experiences

Louis, I think this is the beginning of a beautiful friendship.
—RICK (HUMPHREY BOGART) TO LOUIS (CLAUDE RAINS), in *Casablanca*

We are so fond of each other because our ailments are the same.
—JONATHAN SWIFT, *The Journal to Stella*

Friendship is born at that moment when one person says to another, "What! You, too? I thought I was the only one."

—C. S. LEWIS, "Friendship," The Four Loves

The sharing of joy, whether physical, emotional, psychic, or intellectual, forms a bridge between the sharers which can be the basis for understanding much of what is not shared between them.

—AUDRE LORDE, Sister Outsider: Essays and Speeches

There are some things you can't share without ending up liking each other, and knocking out a twelve-foot mountain troll is one of them.

—J. K. ROWLING, Harry Potter and the Sorcerer's Stone

Love, friendship, respect do not unite people as much as common hatred for something.

—ANTON CHEKOV, Notebooks

One can never speak enough of the virtues, the dangers, the power of shared laughter.

—attributed to FRANCOISE SAGAN

He deserves Paradise who makes his companions laugh.

—THE QUR'AN (KORAN)

And in the sweetness of friendship let there be
    laughter, and sharing of pleasures.
For in the dew of little things the heart finds its
    morning and is refreshed.

—KAHLIL GIBRAN, *The Prophet*

Seven years would be insufficient to make some people acquainted with each other, and seven days are more than enough for others.

—JANE AUSTEN, *Sense and Sensibility*

We were just singing along: "Jeremiah was a bull-frog. Was a good friend of mine. I never understood a single word he said, but I helped him drink his wine." Of course that made perfect sense to us. Why should we question that? We've all had friends who were frogs. We didn't fully understand what they were saying, but if it seemed like that if they wanted you to help them drink some wine, you did it. They would always have some mighty fine wine with 'em too. Frogs could get a hold of that stuff.

—ELLEN DEGENERES, *My Point…And I Do Have One*

There seems to be a peculiar and particular tie between men who have been drunk together.

—ANNE ELLIS, *The Life of an Ordinary Woman*

A man must eat a peck of salt with his friend, before he knows him.

—MIGUEL DE CERVANTES, *Don Quixote*

14

Trust

No soul is desolate as long as there is a human being for whom it can feel trust and reverence.

—attributed to GEORGE ELIOT

If we listened to our intellect...we'd never have a friendship. Well, that's nonsense. You've got to jump off cliffs all the time and build your wings on the way down.

—attributed to RAY BRADBURY

The language of Friendship is not words, but meanings. It is an intelligence above language.

—HENRY DAVID THOREAU,
"A Week on the Concord and Merrimack Rivers"

He's a Blockhead who wants a proof of what
     he Can't Perceive,
And he's a Fool who tries to make such a
     Blockhead believe.

—WILLIAM BLAKE, *Notebooks*

The best and most beautiful things in the world cannot be seen or even touched. They must be felt with the heart.

—attributed to HELEN KELLER

If you treat people right they will treat you right—ninety percent of the time.

—attributed to FRANKLIN DELANO ROOSEVELT

It is more shameful to distrust one's friends than to be deceived by them.

—FRANÇOIS LA ROCHEFOUCAULD, *Maxims*

All men profess honesty as long as they can. To believe all men honest would be folly. To believe none so is something worse.

—attributed to JOHN QUINCY ADAMS

More persons, on the whole, are humbugged by believing in nothing than by believing too much.

—attributed to P. T. BARNUM

To know someone here or there with whom you can feel there is understanding, in spite of distances or thoughts expressed, that can make life a garden.

—attributed to JOHANN WOLFGANG VON GOETHE

Few things help an individual more than to place responsibility upon him, and to let him know that you trust him.

—BOOKER T. WASHINGTON, *Up from Slavery*

Honesty

I praise loudly, I blame softly.

—Catherine the Great of Russia, in a 1794 letter

What is the good of friendship if one cannot say exactly what one means?

—Oscar Wilde, "The Devoted Friend,"
The Happy Prince and Other Tales

May God preserve me from the love of a friend who will never dare to rebuke me.

—Thomas Merton, *No Man Is an Island*

Don't flatter yourself that friendship authorizes you to say disagreeable things to your intimates. The nearer you come into relation with a person, the more necessary do tact and courtesy become.

–OLIVER WENDELL HOLMES,
The Autocrat of the Breakfast-Table

We have those three unspeakably precious things: freedom of speech, freedom of conscience, and the prudence never to practice either.

–MARK TWAIN, *Following the Equator*

Before I can live with other folks I've got to live with myself. The one thing that doesn't abide by majority rule is a person's conscience.

–HARPER LEE, *To Kill a Mockingbird*

The worst crime is faking it.

–KURT COBAIN

This above all: to thine own self be true,
And it must follow, as the night the day,
Thou canst not then be false to any man.

—WILLIAM SHAKESPEARE, *Hamlet*

I'd have this rule that nobody could do anything phony when they visited me. If anybody tried to do anything phony, they couldn't stay.

—J. D. SALINGER, *The Catcher in the Rye*

No person is your friend who demands your silence, or denies your right to grow.

—attributed to ALICE WALKER

It is discouraging how many people are shocked by honesty and how few by deceit.

—attributed to NOEL COWARD

A good friend who points out mistakes and imperfections and rebukes evil is to be respected as if he reveals a secret of hidden treasure.

—BUDDHA,
The Dhammapada: The Path of Perfection

I am always willing to learn. I do not, however, always enjoy being taught.

—attributed to WINSTON LEONARD SPENCER CHURCHILL

Before you criticize someone, you should walk a mile in their shoes. That way, when you criticize them you are a mile away…and you have their shoes.

—AL FRANKEN AS JACK HANDEY, *Deeper Thoughts*

It is wise to apply the oil of refined politeness to the mechanism of friendship.

—COLETTE, *The Pure and the Impure*

Tart Words make no Friends; a Spoonful of Honey will catch more Flies than a Gallon of Vinegar.

—BENJAMIN FRANKLIN, *Poor Richard's Almanack*

I'm going to rub your faces in things you try to avoid. I don't find it strange that all you want to believe in is only that which comforts you. How else do humans invent the traps which betray us into mediocrity? How else do we define cowardice?

—FRANK HERBERT, *Children of Dune*

How can sincerity be a condition of friendship? A taste for truth at any cost is a passion which spares nothing.

—attributed to ALBERT CAMUS

When friends stop being frank and useful to each other, the whole world loses some of its radiance.

—ANATOLE BROYARD

True friendship can afford true knowledge. It does not depend on darkness and ignorance.

—HENRY DAVID THOREAU,
A Week on the Concord and Merrimack Rivers

If you do not tell the truth about yourself you cannot tell it about other people.

—VIRGINIA WOOLF, "The Leaning Tower"

I don't want any yes-men around me. I want everybody to tell me the truth even if it costs them their jobs.

—attributed to SAMUEL GOLDWYN

Support

Sometimes being a friend means mastering the art of timing. There is a time for silence. A time to let go and allow people to hurl themselves into their own destiny. And a time to prepare to pick up the pieces when it's all over.

—attributed to OCTAVIA BUTLER

Never cease loving a person, and never give up hope for him, for even the prodigal son who had fallen most low, could still be saved; the bitterest enemy and also he who was your friend could again be your friend; love that has grown cold can kindle again.

—attributed to SØREN KIERKEGAARD

Thus nature has no love for solitude, and always leans, as it were, on some support; and the sweetest support is found in the most intimate friendship.

—attributed to MARCUS TULLIUS CICERO

The hearts that never lean, must fall.

—EMILY DICKINSON, in a letter, 1881

We cannot live only for ourselves. A thousand fibers connect us with our fellow men; and among those fibers, as sympathetic threads, our actions run as causes, and they come back to us as effects.

—HERMAN MELVILLE

It is a curious thought, but it is only when you see people looking ridiculous that you realize just how much you love them.

—attributed to AGATHA CHRISTIE

Treat your friends as you do your pictures, and place them in their best light.

—JENNIE JEROME CHURCHILL, "Friendship"

Except in cases of necessity, which are rare, leave your friend to learn unpleasant things from his enemies; they are ready enough to tell them.

—OLIVER WENDELL HOLMES,
The Autocrat of the Breakfast-Table

In the end, we will remember not the words of our enemies, but the silence of our friends.

—attributed to REV. DR. MARTIN LUTHER KING, JR.

Anybody can sympathize with the sufferings of a friend, but it requires a very fine nature to sympathize with a friend's success.

—attributed to OSCAR WILDE

One can't complain. I have my friends. Someone spoke to me only yesterday.

—EEYORE, as written by A. A. Milne

It is not so much our friends' help that helps us as the confident knowledge that they will help us.

—attributed to EPICURUS

Friendship is a strong and habitual inclination in two persons to promote the good and happiness of one another.

—EUSTACE BUDGELL, Spectator

What greater thing is there for two human souls, than to feel that they are joined for life—to strengthen each other in all labor, to rest on each other in all sorrow, to minister to each other in all pain, to be with one another in silent unspeakable memories at the moment of the last parting!

—GEORGE ELIOT, Adam Bede

Generosity

From what we get, we can make a living; what we give, however, makes a life.

—ARTHUR ASHE

It is well to give when asked, but it is better to give unasked, through understanding.

—KAHLIL GIBRAN, "On Giving," *The Prophet*

Since you get more joy out of giving joy to others, you should put a good deal of thought into the happiness that you are able to give.

—attributed to ELEANOR ROOSEVELT

Without friends no one would choose to live, though he had all other goods.

—ARISTOTLE, *Nichomachean Ethics*

I feel very close to you all now; so close I could almost … loan you money. Really. It goes that deep.

—attributed to TOM WAITS

Acquaintance: A person whom we know well enough to borrow from, but not well enough to lend to.

—AMBROSE BIERCE, *The Devil's Dictionary*

I'll keep it short and sweet. Family. Religion. Friendship. These are the three demons you must slay if you wish to succeed in business.

—MONTGOMERY BURNS, *The Simpsons*

Business, you know, may bring money, but friendship hardly ever does.

—JANE AUSTEN, Emma

Money can't buy you friends, but it can get you a better class of enemy.

—SPIKE MILLIGAN, Puckoon

O grant me, Heaven, a middle state,
Neither too humble nor too great;
More than enough, for nature's ends,
With something left to treat my friends.

—DAVID MALLET, Imitation of Horace

Kindness in words creates confidence. Kindness in thinking creates profoundness. Kindness in giving creates love.

—LAO TZU, Tao Te Ching

Quirks

Certain flaws are necessary for the whole. It would seem strange if old friends lacked certain quirks.

—attributed to JOHANN WOLFGANG VON GOETHE

People are unreasonable, illogical, and self-centered. Love them anyway.

—MOTHER THERESA, *A Simple Path*

Nobody realizes that some people expend tremendous energy merely to be normal.

—attributed to ALBERT CAMUS

Even among men lacking all distinction he inevitably stood out as a man lacking more distinction than all the rest, and people who met him were always impressed at how unimpressive he was.

—JOSEPH HELLER, *Catch-22*

I have never met a man so ignorant that I couldn't learn something from him.

—attributed to GALILEO GALILEI

Everything that irritates us about others can lead us to an understanding of ourselves.

—CARL JUNG, *Memories, Dreams, Reflections*

It is in pardoning that we are pardoned.

—ST. FRANCIS OF ASSISI, "The Prayer of St. Francis"

Never look down on anybody unless you're helping him up.

—attributed to REV. JESSE JACKSON

'Tis great Confidence in a Friend to tell him your Faults, still greater to tell him his.

—BENJAMIN FRANKLIN, *Poor Richard's Almanack*

Every man should have a fair-sized cemetery in which to bury the faults of his friends.

—attributed to HENRY BROOKS ADAMS

Every murderer is probably somebody's old friend.

—AGATHA CHRISTIE, *The Mysterious Affair at Styles*

A person's flaws are largely what make him or her likable.

—ANN LAMOTT, Bird by Bird

The only people for me are the mad ones, the ones who are mad to live, mad to talk, mad to be saved; the ones who never yawn or say a commonplace thing, but burn, burn, burn, like fabulous yellow Roman candles exploding like spiders across the stars.

—JACK KEROUAC, On the Road

Loyalty

Be slow to fall into friendship; but when thou art in, continue firm and constant.

—attributed to SOCRATES

The friendship between me and you I will not compare to a chain; for that rains might rust, or the falling tree might break.

—WILLIAM PENN, "Treaty with the Indians"

A true friend stabs you in the front.

—OSCAR WILDE

The proper office of a friend is to side with you when you are in the wrong. Nearly anybody will side with you when you are in the right.

—MARK TWAIN, *Mark Twain's Notebook*

We must not confuse dissent with disloyalty.

—EDWARD R. MURROW, as quoted on *See It Now*

Since when do you have to agree with people to defend them from injustice?

—LILLIAN HELLMAN

If I had to choose between betraying my country and betraying my friend, I hope I should have the guts to betray my country.

—E. M. FORSTER, *Two Cheers for Democracy*

Arguments

Perhaps the most delightful friendships are those in which there is much agreement, much disputation, and yet more personal liking.

—attributed to GEORGE ELIOT

"Let's fight till six, and then have dinner," said Tweedledum.

—LEWIS CARROLL, *Through the Looking-Glass*

I dislike arguments of any kind. They are always vulgar, and often convincing.

—OSCAR WILDE, *The Importance of Being Earnest*

Granting that you and I argue, if you get the better of me, and not I of you, are you necessarily right and I wrong? Or if I get the better of you and not you of me, am I necessarily right and you wrong? Or are we both partly right and partly wrong? Or are we both wholly right and wholly wrong? You and I cannot know this, and consequently we all live in darkness.

—CHUANG TZU, *On Leveling All Things*

Love involves a particular unfathomable combination of understanding and misunderstanding.

—attributed to DIANE ARBUS

The greater the contrast, the greater is the potential. Great energy only comes from a correspondingly great tension between opposites.

—attributed to CARL JUNG

Though friendship is not quick to burn,
It is explosive stuff.

> —MAY SARTON,
> "Friendship: The Storms," *A Grain of Mustard Seed*

I was angry with my friend:
I told my wrath, my wrath did end.
I was angry with my foe:
I told it not, my wrath did grow.

> —WILLIAM BLAKE,
> "A Poison Tree," *Songs of Experience*

You lose a lot of time hating people.

> —MARIAN ANDERSON, as quoted in *New York Times*

Life is very short
and there's no time
for fussing and fighting my friends...

> —JOHN LENNON/PAUL MCCARTNEY,
> "With a Little Help from My Friends"

Words and eggs must be handled with care.
Once broken they are impossible
things to repair.

   —Anne Sexton, "Words," *Words for Dr. Y*

Talk little, and Hear much. Reflect alone upon what passed in Company.

   —Thomas Fuller, *Introductio ad Prudentiam*

Silence is argument carried out by other means.

   —attributed to Ernesto "Che" Guevara

Whoever undertakes to set himself up as a judge of Truth and Knowledge is shipwrecked by the laughter of the gods.

   —attributed to Albert Einstein

The smart way to keep people passive and obedient is to strictly limit the spectrum of acceptable opinion, but allow very lively debate within that spectrum—even encourage the more critical and dissident views. That gives people the sense that there's free thinking going on, while all the time the presuppositions of the system are being reinforced by the limits put on the range of the debate.

—Noam Chomsky, *The Common Good*

Many times what cannot be refuted by arguments can be parried by laughter.

—Desiderius Erasmus, *The Praise of Folly*

A "no" uttered from deepest conviction is better and greater than a "yes" merely uttered to please, or what is worse, to avoid trouble.

—attributed to Mohandas Karamchand Gandhi

I think the reward for conformity is everyone likes you but yourself.

—attributed to RITA MAE BROWN

I have opinions of my own—strong opinions—but I don't always agree with them.

—attributed to GEORGE HERBERT WALKER BUSH

In all life one should comfort the afflicted, but verily, also, one should afflict the comfortable, and especially when they are comfortably, contentedly, even happily wrong.

—JOHN KENNETH GALBRAITH

We must love them both—those whose opinions we share and those whose opinions we reject. For both have labored in the search for truth, and both have helped us in the finding of it.

—attributed to ST. THOMAS AQUINAS

Influence

Sometimes our light goes out but is blown again into flame by an encounter with another human being. Each of us owes the deepest thanks to those who have rekindled this inner light.

—attributed to DR. ALBERT SCHWEITZER

Blessed is the influence of one true, loving human soul on another.

—GEORGE ELIOT,
"Janet's Repentance," *Scenes of Clerical Life*

In real friendship the judgment, the genius, the prudence of each party become the common property of both.

—MARIA EDGEWORTH, *Letters of Julia and Caroline*

Neither a lofty degree of intelligence nor imagination nor both together go into the making of genius. Love, love, love, that is the soul of genius.

—attributed to WOLFGANG AMADEUS MOZART

Tell me what company you keep, and I'll tell you what you are.

—MIGUEL DE CERVANTES, *Don Quixote*

Associate yourself with men of good quality if you esteem your own reputation; for 'tis better to be alone than in bad company.

—attributed to GEORGE WASHINGTON

Do not make friends with a hot-tempered man.
Do not associate with one easily angered,
Or you may learn his ways and get yourself
    ensnared.

—THE BIBLE, Proverbs 22:24

One must never judge people by the company they keep: Judas, for example, had irreproachable friends.

—attributed to PAUL VERLAINE

Treat people as if they were what they ought to be and you help them to become what they are capable of being.

—attributed to JOHANN WOLFGANG VON GOETHE

Advice

To give and receive advice—the former with freedom and yet without bitterness, the latter with patience and without irritation—is peculiarly appropriate to genuine friendship.

—CICERO, *De Amicitia*

Human beings, who are almost unique in having the ability to learn from the experience of others, are also remarkable for their apparent disinclination to do so.

—DOUGLAS ADAMS, *Last Chance to See*

Do not use a hatchet to remove a fly from your friend's forehead.

—CHINESE PROVERB

You're not gonna change any of them by talkin' right, they've got to want to learn themselves.

—HARPER LEE, *To Kill a Mockingbird*

Trials

Prosperity provideth, but adversity proveth friends.

—Queen Elizabeth I, 1580

It's a good thing to have all the props pulled out from under us occasionally. It gives us some sense of what is rock under our feet, and what is sand.

—Madeline L'Engle,
The Summer of the Great-Grandmother

A real friend is one who walks in when the rest of the world walks out.

—attributed to Walter Winchell

True friendship is a plant of slow growth, and must undergo and withstand the shocks of adversity before it is entitled to the appellation.

—George Washington, in a 1783 letter

In the face of a true friend a man sees, as it were, a second self. So that where his friend is he is; if his friend be rich, he is not poor; though he be weak, his friend's strength is his; and in his friend's life he enjoys a second life after his own is finished.

—Cicero, "On Friendship"

Greater love hath no man than this, that he lay down his life for his friends.

—The Bible, John 15:13

The ultimate measure of a man is not where he stands in moments of comfort and convenience, but where he stands at times of challenge and controversy.

—Rev. Dr. Martin Luther King, Jr.,
Strength to Love

Whenever a friend succeeds, a little something in me dies.

—Gore Vidal

Human relations are not fixed in their orbits like the planets—they're more like galaxies, changing all the time, exploding into light for years, then dying away.

—May Sarton, *Crucial Conversations*

People change and forget to tell each other.

—Lillian Hellman, *Toys in the Attic*

Much unhappiness has come into the world because of bewilderment and things left unsaid.

—FYODOR DOSTOEVSKY, "Critical Articles"

The easiest kind of relationship for me is with ten thousand people. The hardest is with one.

—attributed to JOAN BAEZ

I think the mistake a lot of us make is thinking the state-appointed psychiatrist is our "friend."

—AL FRANKEN as Jack Handey, *Deeper Thoughts*

True friendship is never serene.

—MARIE DE RABUTIN-CHANTAL, Marquise de Sévigné

Comfort

What do we live for, if it is not to make life less dif-
ficult for each other?

—attributed to GEORGE ELIOT

Friend,
don't cry
with the moon of your face
turned away.
Love's ways are like this:
as curled as the tendrils
of new cucumber.

—HLA STAVHANA, *The Gthsaptaat of Stavhana Hla*

I felt it shelter to speak to you.

—EMILY DICKINSON, in a letter, 1878

So long as we are loved by others I should say that we are almost indispensable; and no man is useless while he has a friend.

—ROBERT LOUIS STEVENSON,
"Lay Morals," *Across the Plains*

I find it hard to believe you don't know the
    beauty you are.
But if you don't, let me be your eyes,
A hand to your darkness, so you won't be afraid.

—LOU REED, "I'll Be Your Mirror"

Best friend, my wellspring in the wilderness!

—GEORGE ELIOT, *The Spanish Gypsy*

If you want others to be happy, practice compassion. If you want to be happy, practice compassion.

—attributed to TENZIN GYATSO, 14th Dalai Lama

How far you go in life depends on your being tender with the young, compassionate with the aged, sympathetic with the striving and tolerant of the weak and strong. Because someday in life you will have been all of these.

—GEORGE WASHINGTON CARVER, in a 1920 interview

Kind words are easy and short to speak, but their echoes are truly endless.

—attributed to MOTHER THERESA

Some people go to priests; others to poetry; I to my friends.

—VIRGINIA WOOLF, *The Waves*

Upkeep

Love doesn't just sit there, like a stone; it has to be made, like bread; re-made all the time, made new.

—URSULA K. LEGUIN, *The Lathe of Heaven*

When I get older, losing my hair
many years from now,
Will you still be sending me a valentine,
Birthday greetings, bottle of wine?

—JOHN LENNON/PAUL MCCARTNEY,
"When I'm Sixty-Four"

I do not wish to treat friendships daintily, but with the roughest courage. When they are real, they are not glass threads or frost-work, but the solidest thing we know.

—RALPH WALDO EMERSON,
"Friendship," *Essays, First Series*

There is nothing in the world I wouldn't do for Bob Hope, and there is nothing he wouldn't do for me. We spend our lives doing nothing for each other.

—attributed to BING CROSBY

Friendship is never established as an understood relation. It is a miracle which requires constant proofs. It is an exercise of the purest imagination and of the rarest faith!

—HENRY DAVID THOREAU,
A Week on the Concord and Merrimack Rivers

Love thyself last. Look near, behold thy duty
To those who walk beside thee down life's road;
Make glad their days by little acts of beauty,
And help them bear the burden of earth's load.

—ELLA WHEELER WILCOX, "Love Thyself Last"

Keep your friends close, but keep your enemies closer.

—AL PACINO, in *The Godfather, Part II*

I have lost friends, some by death…and some by a sheer inability to cross the street.

—VIRGINIA WOOLF, *The Waves*

Friends in Need

Your friend is your needs answered.
For you come to him with your hunger, and you
    seek him for peace.
When your friend speaks his mind you fear not
    the "nay" in your mind, nor do you withhold
    the "ay."
And let your best be for your friend.
If he must know the ebb of your tide, let him
    know its flood also.

—KAHLIL GIBRAN, *The Prophet*

He that is thy friend indeed
He will help thee in thy need.

      —WILLIAM SHAKESPEARE, *The Passionate Pilgrim*

Think twice before you speak to a friend in need.

      —AMBROSE BIERCE, *The Devil's Dictionary*

Be more prompt to go to a friend in adversity than in prosperity.

      —attributed to CHILO (C. 560 B.C.)

It's the friends you can call at four A.M. that matter.

      —attributed to MARLENE DIETRICH

The friend who holds your hand and says the wrong thing is made of dearer stuff than the one who stays away.

      —BARBARA KINGSOLVER,
      High Tide in Tucson: Essays from Now or Never

If a friend of mine gave a feast, and did not invite me to it, I should not mind a bit. But if a friend of mine had a sorrow and refused to allow me to share it, I should feel it most bitterly. If he shut the doors of the house of mourning against me, I would move back again and again and beg to be admitted so that I might share in what I was entitled to share. If he thought me unworthy, unfit to weep with him, I should feel it as the most poignant humiliation.

—OSCAR WILDE, *De Profundis*

Walking with a friend in the dark is better than walking alone in the light.

—attributed to HELEN KELLER

Friends and Lovers

Love is like the wild rose-briar,
Friendship like the holly-tree—
The holly is dark when the rose-briar blooms
But which will bloom most constantly?

—EMILY BRONTË, *Wuthering Heights*

Friendship is constant in all other things
Save in the office and affairs of love.

—WILLIAM SHAKESPEARE, *Much Ado about Nothing.*

Friendship, which is of its nature a delicate thing, fastidious, slow of growth, is easily checked, will hesitate, demur, recoil where love, good old blustering love, bowls ahead and blunders through every obstacle.

—COLETTE, *My Apprenticeships*

Friendship has splendors that love knows not. It grows stronger when crossed, whereas obstacles kill love. Friendship resists time, which wearies and severs couples. It has heights unknown to love.

—MARIAMA BÂ, *So Long a Letter*

The best friend will probably get the best spouse, because a good marriage is based on the talent for friendship.

—FRIEDRICH NIETZSCHE, "Friendship and Marriage"

We may generally conclude the Marriage of a Friend to be the Funeral of a Friendship.

—Katherine Philips

The end
of passion
may refashion
a friend.

—Mona Van Duyn, "The Beginning," *Firefall*

Friendships are easy to get out of compared to love affairs, but they are not easy to get out of compared to, say, jail.

—Fran Leibowitz

Friendship is certainly the finest balm for the pangs of disappointed love.

—Jane Austen, *Northanger Abbey*

However rare true love is in a marriage, true friendship is rarer.

—FRANÇOIS LA ROCHEFOUCAULD, *Maxims*

Old Friends

I have come to esteem history as a component of friendships. In my case at least friendships are not igneous but sedimentary.

—JANE HOWARD, *Please Touch*

Among my friends love is a wage
that one might have for an honest living.

—ROBERT DUNCAN

Champagne for my real friends, real pain for my sham friends.

—attributed to TOM WAITS

Even where the affections are not strongly moved by any superior excellence, the companions of our childhood always possess a certain power over our minds which hardly any later friend can obtain.

—MARY SHELLEY, *Frankenstein*

Good old Watson! You are the one fixed point in a changing age.

—SHERLOCK HOLMES,
in Sir Arthur Conan Doyle's *His Last Bow*

My coat and I live comfortably together. It has has molded assumed all my wrinkles, does not hurt me anywhere, itself on my deformities, and is complacent to all my movements, and I only feel its presence because it keeps me warm. Old coats and old friends are the same thing.

—VICTOR HUGO, *Les Misérables*

Grow old along with me!
The best is yet to be,
The last of life, for which the first is made.

—ROBERT BROWNING, Dramatis Personae

We are not the same persons this year as last; nor are those we love. It is a happy chance if we, changing, continue to love a changed person.

—attributed to W. SOMERSET MAUGHAM

New Friends

Old friends pass away, new friends appear. It is just like the days. An old day passes, a new day arrives. The important thing is to make it meaningful: a meaningful friend—or a meaningful day.

—attributed to TENZIN GYATSO, 14th Dalai Lama

I have lost my seven best friends, which is to say that God has had mercy on me seven times without realizing it. He lent a friendship, took it from me, and sent me another.

JEAN COCTEAU

If a man does not make new acquaintance as he advances through life, he will soon find himself left alone. A man, sir, should keep his friendship in constant repair.

—SAMUEL JOHNSON

True friendship's laws are by this rule express'd,
Welcome the coming, speed the parting guest.

—HOMER, *The Odyssey*

Those friends thou hast, and their adoption tried,
Grapple them to thy soul with hoops of steel;
But do not dull thy palm with entertainment
Of each new–hatch'd, unfledg'd comrade.

—WILLIAM SHAKESPEARE, *Hamlet*

Faraway Friends

What can melt a traveler's grief?
Opening your letter I see the words in your fine
    hand.
...I hide this letter in a scented box,
And when I'm sad, I take it out again.

—Yu Xuanji (c. 9th century B.C.)

Sir, more than kisses, letters, mingle souls; for thus,
absent friends speak.

—John Donne, in a 1598 letter

Like everyone else I feel the need of relations and friendship, of affection, of friendly intercourse, and I am not made of stone or iron, so I cannot miss these things without feeling, as does any other intelligent man, a void and deep need. I tell you this to let you know how much good your visit has done me.

—Vincent Van Gogh

How I wish you were here.
We're just two lost souls
swimming in a fish bowl year after year...

—Pink Floyd, "Wish You Were Here,"
by David Gilmour and Roger Waters

Where you used to be, there is a hole in the world, which I find myself constantly walking around in the daytime and falling into at night. I miss you like hell.

—Edna St. Vincent Millay, *Letters*

When you part from your friend, you grieve not;
For that which you love most in him
may be clearer in his absence,
as the mountain to the climber
is clearer from the plain.

—Kahlil Gibran, "On Friendship," *The Prophet*

Here at the frontier, there are falling leaves.
Although my neighbors are all barbarians,
And you, you are a thousand miles away,
There are always two cups on my table.

—Anonymous Tang Dynasty poet (c. 618-906 A.D.)

Friendship is the greatest of worldly goods.
Certainly to me it is the chief happiness of life.
If I had to give a piece of advice to a young
man about a place to live, I think I should say,
"Sacrifice almost everything to live where you can
be near your friends."

—C. S. Lewis,
The Letters of C. S. Lewis to Arthur Greeves

I returned
from
archipelagos,
I returned from jasmine
and deserts
to simply being
simply being
simply being
with other beings
and when I was no longer a shadow
and no longer on the run
when I was fully human, I received the freight
of the human heart...

—PABLO NERUDA,
"Ode to My Sorrows," *Odes to Opposites*

Without Friends

It seems to me that trying to live without friends is like milking a bear to get cream for your morning coffee. It is a whole lot of trouble, and then not worth much after you get it.

—ZORA NEALE HURSTON, *Dust Tracks on a Road*

Only solitary men know the full joys of friendship. Others have their family; but to a solitary and an exile his friends are everything.

—WILLA CATHER, *Shadows on the Rock*

If we have no peace, it is because we have forgotten that we belong to each other.

—attributed to MOTHER TERESA

I wish my deadly foe, no worse
Than want of friends, and an empty purse.

—NICHOLAS BRETON, "A Farewell to Town"

There is no agony like bearing an untold story inside of you.

—attributed to MAYA ANGELOU

The worst solitude is to be destitute of sincere friendship.

—FRANCIS BACON,
De Dignitate et Augmentis Scientiarum

"Stay" is a charming word in a friend's vocabulary.

—attributed to LOUISA MARY ALCOTT

In Good Company

However deep our devotion may be to parents, or to children, it is our contemporaries alone with whom understanding is instinctive and entire.

—VERA BRITTAIN, *Testament of Youth*

God gave us our relatives—thank God we can choose our friends.

—ETHEL WATTS MUMFORD, *The Cynic's Calendar*

We are not permitted to choose the frame of our destiny. But what we put into it is ours.

—DAG HAMMERSKJÖLD, *Markings*

Even in a time of elephantine vanity and greed, one never has to look far to see the campfires of gentle people.

—GARRISON KEILLOR,
We Are Still Married: Stories and Letters

There is no safety in numbers, or in anything else.

—JAMES THURBER, "The Fairly Intelligent Fly"

Friendships multiply Joys and divide Griefs.

—THOMAS FULLER, *Gnomologia: Adages and Proverbs*

One loyal friend is worth ten thousand relatives.

—attributed to EURIPIDES (c. 408 B.C.)

I have always depended on the kindness of strangers.

—Tennessee Williams, *Streetcar Named Desire*

I don't know half of you half as well as I should like; and I like less than half of you half as well as you deserve.

—J. R. R. Tolkien, *The Hobbit*

The happiest moments my heart knows are those in which it is pouring forth its affections to a few esteemed characters.

—attributed to Thomas Jefferson

There is no hope of joy except in human relations.

—attributed to Antoine de Saint-Exupéry

Gratitude

It is not our purpose to become each other; it is to recognize each other, to learn to see the other and honor him for what he is.

—HERMAN HESSE, *Demian*

A coward is incapable of exhibiting love; it is the prerogative of the brave.

—attributed to MOHANDAS KARAMCHAND GANDHI

People think love is an emotion. Love is good sense.

—KEN KESEY

When you have seen the glow of happiness on the face of a beloved person, you know that a man can have no vocation but to awaken that light on the faces surrounding him.

—ALBERT CAMUS

Let us be grateful to people who make us happy; they are the charming gardeners who make our souls blossom.

—MARCEL PROUST, *Remembrance of Things Past*

My friends are my estate.

—EMILY DICKINSON

From quiet homes and first beginning,
Out to the undiscovered ends,
There's nothing worth the wear of winning,
But laughter and the love of friends.

—HILAIRE BELLOC, *Verses*

I no doubt deserved my enemies, but I don't
believe I deserved my friends.

—WALT WHITMAN, *Leaves of Grass*

You have been my friend. That in itself is a tremendous thing. I wove my webs for you because I liked
you. After all, what's a life, anyway? We're born, we
live a little while, we die. A spider's life can't help
being something of a mess, with all this trapping
and eating flies. By helping you, perhaps I was
trying to lift up my life a trifle. Heaven knows
anyone's life can stand a little of that.

—E. B. WHITE, *Charlotte's Web*

We are each other's harvest;
we are each other's business;
we are each other's magnitude and bond.

—GWENDOLYN BROOKS

Never shall I forget the time I spent with you. Please continue to be my friend, as you will always find me yours.

—LUDWIG VAN BEETHOVEN

All these places have their moments
With lovers and friends I still can recall
Some are dead and some are living
In my life I loved them all.

—JOHN LENNON/PAUL MCCARTNEY, "In My Life"

Between the earth and sky
I draw a map for the newcomer.
Before I die
I give him his inheritance:
the glow of love,
a ladder and a living room full of friends.

—SAMI MAHDI, "The Inheritance"

Always go to other people's funerals, otherwise they won't come to yours—and think how that'll make you feel.

—Yogi Berra

My friends have made the story of my life. In a thousand ways they have turned my limitations into beautiful privileges, and enabled me to walk serene and happy in the shadow cast by my deprivation.

—Helen Keller, *The Story of My Life*

Think where man's glory most begins and ends
And say my glory was I had such friends.

—W. B. Yeats "The Municipal Gallery"